The Magic *of* Christmas

DUETS FOR PIANO
Arranged by Dennis Alexander

Christmas is truly a time of sharing, and expressing the beauty and wonder of the Christmas season through music is an experience which provides many happy memories for years to come. These special duet arrangements are meant to please both young and old, and will provide the "perfect touch" for a Christmas recital or informal gathering. Both parts are musically interesting and rewarding to play. The words for each selection are also included so that friends and family may sing along and share the "Magic of Christmas." Have fun, and Merry Christmas to all of you!

Dennis Alexander

© Copyright MCMLXXXVIII by Alfred Publishing Co., Inc.

SILENT NIGHT

Silent night, holy night, All is calm, all is bright.
Round yon Virgin mother and Child, Holy Infant so tender and mild,
Sleep in heavenly peace, Sleep in heavenly peace.

Joseph Mohr

Franz Gruber

Andante moderato

SILENT NIGHT

Silent night, holy night, All is calm, all is bright.
Round yon Virgin mother and Child, Holy Infant so tender and mild,
Sleep in heavenly peace, Sleep in heavenly peace.

Joseph Mohr

Franz Gruber

Andante moderato

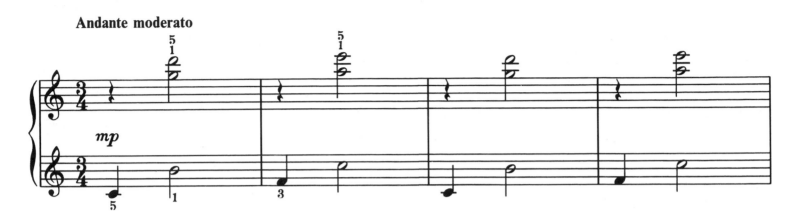

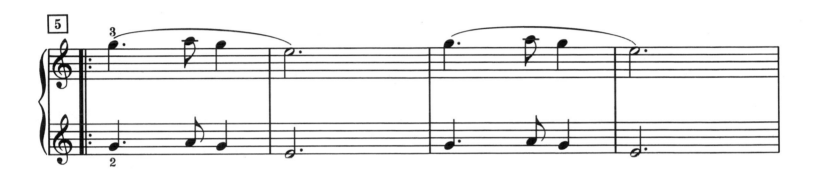

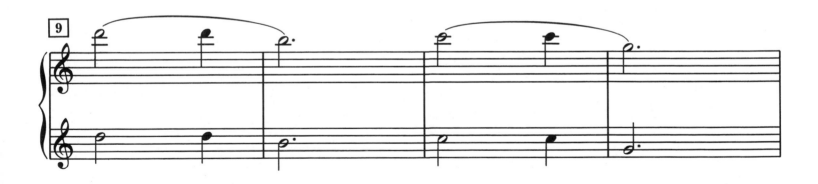

4

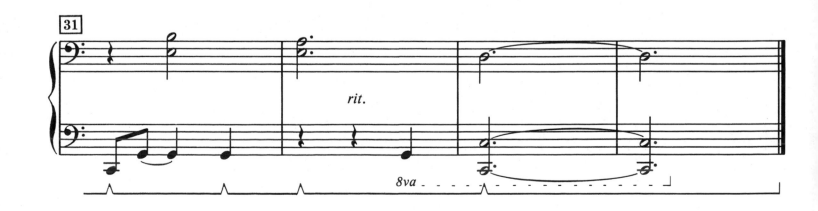

Primo

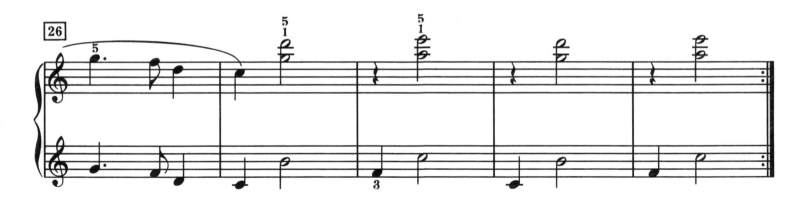

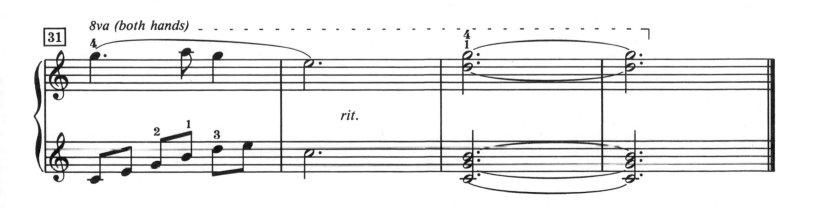

JINGLE BELLS

Dashing through the snow in a one-horse open sleigh,
O'er the fields we go, laughing all the way.
Bells on bobtails ring, making spirits bright,
What fun it is to ride and sing a sleighing song tonight!

Oh, jingle bells, jingle bells, jingle all the way;
Oh, what fun it is to ride in a one-horse open sleigh.

James Pierpont

JINGLE BELLS

Dashing through the snow in a one-horse open sleigh,
O'er the fields we go, laughing all the way.
Bells on bobtails ring, making spirits bright,
What fun it is to ride and sing a sleighing song tonight!

Oh, jingle bells, jingle bells, jingle all the way;
Oh, what fun it is to ride in a one-horse open sleigh.

James Pierpont

Secondo

Primo

SLEEP, LITTLE JESUS

Sleep, little Jesus, my treasure, my blessing.
While Mary comforts Thee, tender, caressing.
Lullaby, little one, in loving arms lying,
Guarding my darling and stilling Thy crying.

Polish

This beautiful melody is one of the many Polish folk tunes adapted by Chopin.
It appears in his Scherzo in B minor.

SLEEP, LITTLE JESUS

Sleep, little Jesus, my treasure, my blessing.
While Mary comforts Thee, tender, caressing.
Lullaby, little one, in loving arms lying,
Guarding my darling and stilling Thy crying.

Polish

This beautiful melody is one of the many Polish folk tunes adapted by Chopin.
It appears in his Scherzo in B minor.

Secondo

Primo

HARK! THE HERALD ANGELS SING

Hark! the herald angels sing, "Glory to the newborn King;
Peace on earth, and mercy mild, God and sinners reconciled!"
Joyful all ye nations, rise, Join the triumph of the skies;
With th'angelic host proclaim, "Christ is born in Bethlehem!"
Hark! the herald angels sing, "Glory to the newborn King."

Charles Wesley

Felix Mendelssohn

HARK! THE HERALD ANGELS SING

Hark! the herald angels sing, "Glory to the newborn King;
Peace on earth, and mercy mild, God and sinners reconciled!"
Joyful all ye nations, rise, Join the triumph of the skies;
With th'angelic host proclaim, "Christ is born in Bethlehem!"
Hark! the herald angels sing, "Glory to the newborn King."

Charles Wesley

Felix Mendelssohn

Allegro ♩=138

Secondo

Primo

WHAT CHILD IS THIS?

(Greensleeves)

William Dix

What Child is this Who laid to rest, on Mary's lap is sleeping?
Whom angels greet with anthems sweet, while shepherds watch are keeping?
This, this is Christ the King, Whom shepherds guard and angels sing:
Haste, haste to bring Him laud, the Babe, the Son of Mary.

English

Andante moderato

WHAT CHILD IS THIS?
(Greensleeves)

William Dix

What Child is this Who laid to rest, on Mary's lap is sleeping?
Whom angels greet with anthems sweet, while shepherds watch are keeping?
This, this is Christ the King, Whom shepherds guard and angels sing:
Haste, haste to bring Him laud, the Babe, the Son of Mary.

English

Andante moderato

Secondo

Primo

ANGELS WE HAVE HEARD ON HIGH

Angels we have heard on high, sweetly singing o'er the plains,
And the mountains in reply, echoing their joyous strains.
Gloria in excelsis Deo, Gloria in excelsis Deo.

French

ANGELS WE HAVE HEARD ON HIGH

Angels we have heard on high, sweetly singing o'er the plains,
And the mountains in reply, echoing their joyous strains.
Gloria in excelsis Deo, Gloria in excelsis Deo.

French

Allegro moderato ♩ = 120

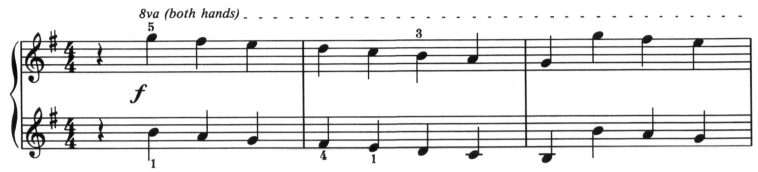

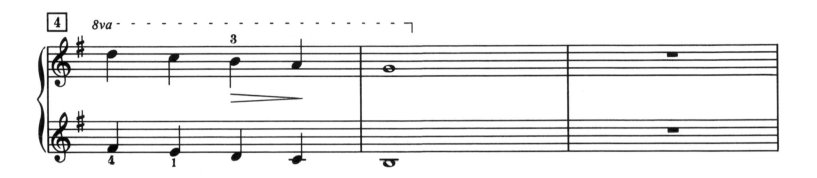

24

Secondo

Primo

THE FIRST NOËL

The first Noël, the angel did say,
Was to certain poor shepherds in fields as they lay;
In fields where they lay keeping their sheep,
On a cold winter's night that was so deep:
Noël, Noël, Noël, Noël, Born is the King of Israel.

English

THE FIRST NOËL

The first Noël, the angel did say,
Was to certain poor shepherds in fields as they lay;
In fields where they lay keeping their sheep,
On a cold winter's night that was so deep:
Noël, Noël, Noël, Noël, Born is the King of Israel.

English

28

Secondo

WE WISH YOU A MERRY CHRISTMAS

We wish you a merry Christmas, We wish you a merry Christmas,
We wish you a merry Christmas and a happy New Year.
Good tidings we bring to you and your kin,
Good tidings for Christmas and a happy New Year.

English

WE WISH YOU A MERRY CHRISTMAS

We wish you a merry Christmas, We wish you a merry Christmas,
We wish you a merry Christmas and a happy New Year.
Good tidings we bring to you and your kin,
Good tidings for Christmas and a happy New Year.

English

Secondo

Primo